T0065790

OUR LIVES
IN VERSE
Everyday Poetry

Ann Brubaker Greenleaf Wirtz

WESTBOW
P R E S S®
A DIVISION OF THOMAS NELSON
& ZONDERVAN

Copyright © 2022 Ann Brubaker Greenleaf Wirtz.

All rights reserved. No part of this book may be used or reproduced by
any means, graphic, electronic, or mechanical, including photocopying,
recording, taping or by any information storage retrieval system
without the written permission of the author except in the case of
brief quotations embodied in critical articles and reviews.

This book is a work of non-fiction. Unless otherwise noted, the author
and the publisher make no explicit guarantees as to the accuracy of
the information contained in this book and in some cases, names of
people and places have been altered to protect their privacy.

WestBow Press books may be ordered through booksellers or by contacting:

WestBow Press
A Division of Thomas Nelson & Zondervan
1663 Liberty Drive
Bloomington, IN 47403
www.westbowpress.com
844-714-3454

Because of the dynamic nature of the Internet, any web addresses or
links contained in this book may have changed since publication and
may no longer be valid. The views expressed in this work are solely those
of the author and do not necessarily reflect the views of the publisher,
and the publisher hereby disclaims any responsibility for them.

Any people depicted in stock imagery provided by Getty Images are
models, and such images are being used for illustrative purposes only.
Certain stock imagery © Getty Images.

Scripture quotations marked (NASB) taken from the (NASB®) New American
Standard Bible®, Copyright © 1960, 1971, 1977, 1995, 2020 by The Lockman
Foundation. Used by permission. All rights reserved. www.lockman.org

Scripture marked (NKJV) taken from the New King James Version®. Copyright
© 1982 by Thomas Nelson. Used by permission. All rights reserved.

Scripture quotations marked (NIV) are taken from the Holy Bible, New
International Version®, NIV®. Copyright © 1973, 1978, 1984, 2011 by Biblica,
Inc.® Used by permission of Zondervan. All rights reserved worldwide.
www.zondervan.com The "NIV" and "New International Version" are trademarks
registered in the United States Patent and Trademark Office by Biblica, Inc.®

Scripture marked (KJV) taken from the King James Version of the Bible.

ISBN: 978-1-6642-7639-0 (sc)
ISBN: 978-1-6642-7638-3 (e)

Print information available on the last page.

WestBow Press rev. date: 09/15/2022

Dedicated to
Patrick
My dearest husband, ever my encourager ...

To
My WOW Writers' Group
Betsy, Carol, Karin, Leanna, Sunny
Who never gave up on me ...

To
Anne and Bob & Lynn and Ronald
Friends dear to my heart ...

And to
Arie Todd, Dewa, Divya, Aarush
My dearest, most precious family ...

Deeply grateful to all.

HOW THIS BOOK CAME TO BE

As a baby boomer who grew up on classical literature and fun and inspiring poetry, I have ever enjoyed the play of words. Over the years, musings made their way to pen and paper, later to keyboard and computer. They were expressions of my life experience. Some writings told the accounts of others.

Underlying all my literary endeavors was a passion to observe, comprehend, and embrace the everyday. I wrote to clarify my thoughts. How does my faith interact with all that happens? How do I respond to the hurts ... the joys ... the fears ... the overwhelming beauty ... the delight found in even the simplest things?

Our Lives in Verse, Everyday Poetry is my contemplative journey in poetic form. Enjoy this sincere, yet playful offering.

July 2022
Ann Brubaker Greenleaf Wirtz

Finally, brothers and sisters, whatever is true, whatever is honorable, whatever is right, whatever is pure, whatever is lovely, whatever is commendable, if there is any excellence and if anything worthy of praise, think about these things (Philippians 4:8 NASB).

CONTENTS

MONTHS OF
THE YEAR

A JANUARY SNOWFALL, AT LAST

January had either been
Too warm for snow
Or the moisture wasn't there,
A disappointment for one such as me,
Who delights in falling flakes,
And snow-covered land
As far as the eye can see.

But this morning at half past nine
Tiny flakes began to fall,
And dashing out to confirm such a sight,
Excited as any child could be,
I laughed with joy and stood in awe
As the snow came down
And covered me.

Large flakes soon filled the pewter sky
And turned the world a wondrous white,
First feathering each branch
On the green holly tree,
Then coating the sidewalk,
Fence and shrub
Till in inches, almost three.

I peered out the windows all-the-day
At the snow that was finally falling,
Enraptured by the silent world
That ever grew before me,
My gratitude awash
In heartfelt prayer,
"To God, be all the glory!"

FEBRUARY'S WARMTH

The warmth of February
Is not found in the daily temperature,
Often a fluctuating read
Between cold and not-so-cold.

It is obviously not found in
A day's chilly rain or
A night's winter snowfall,
Or in a mix of the two that ices the land.

February's warmth, instead, occurs
In our hearts and
In our homes,
And in the south's sunniest climes.

In our homes
The hearth's merry blaze,
With its mesmerizing dance,
Livens our February days.

Its warmth and good cheer
Fellowship with cozy fleece
And steaming mug,
Our comforts enhanced by print.

Then mid-way through this winter month
Comes Valentine's Day,
With roses of red and sentimental cards,
And gifts that heat our embrace.

As messengers of affection,
These traditional offerings
Supplant the weather's chill,
Joyful harbingers of winter's end.

Residents of the sunshine belt
May cherish their balmy, year-round temps,
But the warmth of heart and hearth alone
Uniquely satisfy the rest.

MARCH COLORS

Happily, we smile upon
The triumphant crocus,
Deep purple, brilliant gold,
Some a pale lavender,
The first to poke their sleepy heads
Above the warming soil,
Friends with the arching forsythia,
Its yellow branches waving us forward
Into the season of renewal.

Joyfully, we gaze upon
The cheerful daffodil,
Bright lemon bugler,
Playing its reveille to awaken the land,
For spring has arrived
With its verdant touch accented by
The bold grape hyacinth, a companion
To the vibrant tulip, with
Sweet viola eager to join the symphony.

Breathtakingly, we feast our eyes upon
The weeping cherry,
Long, graceful arms hued in soft pink,
While delicately flowered trees
Line the boulevard and dot the landscape
In a profusion of pastel rose and white,
Complimenting the majestic magnolia and the
elegant redbud,
All nature coming alive
In colorful, springtime glory.

APRIL LACE

Do you see it,
White lace vivid
Against a leafless forest, still brown,
Yet coming to life
With the greening of spring?

Do you gaze intently
To observe four white petals
Centered with a golden
Crown of thorns,
The dogwood blossom, a crucifer of faith?

Do you know
The Easter legend about this lovely tree,
Its branches lifted upward,
The beauty of its flower
Gracing the land like fine lace?

Once a large tree, sturdy as the oak,
Its wood formed the cross of Christ,
It is said, and from this shame both
Curse and blessing came from God, now,
A small, crooked tree with an exquisite blossom,
the cross.

And on each petal's tip a piercing,
The indentation a nail from Calvary,
Touched with the faint red blood of Christ,
His sacrifice we behold
In the aching beauty of the dogwood flower.

Dear Soul, do you see it,
White lace vivid all around,
In neighborhood and forest land,
And understand it's the story of Jesus
Revealed through the bloom we hold in our hand?

PEONIES IN MAY

Bordering the long, grassy driveway
That ran alongside our
Fairview Avenue home,
Next to the old wire fence
That was staked years past
To establish the boundary
Between two neighboring houses,
Peonies bloomed gloriously
Without fail every May.

As then, when the greenish buds
First begin to swell,
Ants dine happily on
The secretion of the peony's sweet nectar,
And while seemingly pesky,
They also make a meal
Of other insects seeking
To do harm, and are therefore
Natural defenders of this flower.

And a good thing, too,
Because a world without
The winsome peony
Would be a sad loss of artistry,
For the world needs
The charming elegance
Of this gentle flower,
With its garden palette
Of light pink, fuchsia, and rose.

An old-fashioned bloom
Even in the 1950s and '60s
When growing up in our
Webster Groves, Missouri, home,
The peony is still a nostalgic staple,
Especially in Midwestern gardens.
But perhaps one of the most
Poignant settings for the ubiquitous
Peony is in an old, small-town cemetery.

This silent world, except for bird song
Trilling and chirping merrily
From stalwart oaks and hardy maples,
Welcomes a contemplative stroll and pause
Before headstones, grand and small.
Names and dates tweak the imagination,
The older the better, with one unusual name
In East Hill Cemetery, Morgantown, Indiana,
Never forgotten: Ophoeba Saltcorn, 1826-1895.

Years ago, two things were tucked away
From evening walks through East Hill,
The profusion of pale pink peony bushes
Dotting the landscape, respectful as sentinels,
And Ophoeba's very distinctive name.
The two intertwine in sweet memory
Of the time lived in Indiana,
Of the soothing peace received
From the eloquence of this tranquil site.

The gladsome peony
Plays on our heartstrings
With remembrances of youth and
Other numerous indelible moments

When living and loveliness overlapped,
Our musings replete with visions of
Peonies nodding in a springtime breeze,
Or centered on a table in a cut-glass vase,
A grace note playing through our memories.

JUNE IN THE MIDDLE

Memorial Day behind us,
The Fourth of July ahead,
Two days so vastly different ...
One somber,
One joyous ...
Yet, of each it can be said,
These days celebrate the best of us:
With tears for the fallen,
The brave who have died,
And cheers for the fireworks
That light the night sky.
Two holidays to honor
The joy and the pain,
To win freedom, so precious ...
A cost with every gain.

And now we pause between the two,
The month of June is here.
Spring turns to summer,
Shimmer to shine ...
Surprise,
We're half-way
Through the year!

Dear Heavenly Father,
Day upon day upon day ... and time goes slowly
by until something is over ... and then how quickly it
passed ... the hours, the days, the weeks, the months ... the
long years ... all go by in haste. Nothing makes that clearer

than history itself, so soon accomplished both in individual lives and nationally in a country's historic sweep. We thank you for the founding of our great nation, America, for every sacrifice in lives and hardship to right wrongs and secure freedom ... our never-ending story. Thank you for every month and year that passes, may we never take life for granted. Bless and keep us today, ever in your care.
In Your Holy Name.
Amen.

Invocation Poem and Prayer
Henderson County Genealogical and Historical Society
Hendersonville, North Carolina
June 2, 2018

JULY IN MY HEART

I firmly attach a bow
To my front porch wreath,
Blue, white and red checked,
Accented with flowers the same,
To make a statement clear:
The Fourth of July is here!

I thoughtfully appraise my table,
Yellow roses for June,
My dining room awaiting
July's monthly theme,
Which, of course, to be true
Is always red, white and blue!

I purposely choose a basket
Lightly detailed with stars
To hold simple white daisies,
Sweet companions to the red and blue
Of other flowers arranged to say,
"Celebrate your freedom today!"

I eagerly reach for pitchers
From my top cupboard shelf,
Functional with graceful lines,
Pleasing with the basket and artful, too,
My treasured collection both new and old,
Their journeyed stories now lost and untold!

I carefully angle my tablecloth,
Homespun blue and patterned with white,
A family favorite for many a year,

Memorable for its summertime use,
A reliable feature in my décor,
Sold years ago, in our own gift store!

I reverently place a runner
To receive the festive array,
Handstitched fabric, an heirloom
In strips shaded blue, white, and red,
Sewn by my local Curb Market friend,
As her creative life approached its end!

I deliberately bought this treasure
As cancer was taking its toll,
Lavon purposefully living
With her head gaily covered, and
Her spirit filled with faith,
Loveliness she continued to create!

I poignantly consider
All this month means,
Patriotism for our country revered, and
Personal events, life-changing with loss,
My first husband, Arie, died from cancer, as well,
This disease a heartbreak, as so many can tell!

Indeed, July has a place in my heart
With its history and beauty,
With its flowers and sorrows,
With nostalgic thoughts of childhood play
So long ago in summer's twilight,
Dear memories of life forever held tight!

AUGUST TRANSITION

In the Northern Hemisphere
Morning light comes later now,
No longer bright at six a.m., but dark,
And an earlier evening descends
As the earth in its spinning orbit of the sun,
With its tilted and unchanging axis, finds
The sun's rays less direct on the North Pole,
Moving us closer to the autumnal equinox.

Within the green woodland
Signs of fall quietly appear,
In the South dogwood trees lighten
With an aura that shades to crimson,
And in the North touches of yellow and red
Flame amongst the hemlock,
As leaves land here and there,
Signaling both an end and a beginning.

Along the traveled byway
The black-eyed Susan wildflower
Winks joyfully in the summer breeze,
And sunflowers stand tall in garden plot
Or farmer's field, grown for beauty
And for the harvest of their seeds,
A favorite for the ever-hungry birds,
Affecting with their avian song and flashing
feathers.

To our alert ears
The rolling buzz and click of the cicada's tymbals
Is the sound of summer, intensifying in August,

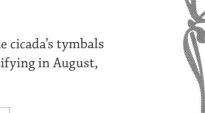

A background anthem accompanying a stroll in the garden
To admire lantana, alive with multi-hued loveliness,
Or impatiens, with colorful wide-open faces, and
Begonias, lavish in shades of serene pink, while
Bright marigolds nestle near queenly red geraniums,
exquisite, all.

Seasons come and soon enough they go,
Be it through the world's natural turn
Or as periods of challenging time,
Even as the gentle passage of our own years,
Rails they are, as seasons frame and steer our lives,
Sometimes along a course we never imagined,
But always in the looking back,
How quickly it all went.

SEPTEMBER AND OCTOBER, A PATCHWORK TAPESTRY

For many of us,
September and October
Usher in a two-month
Wonderland of color,
Sight and sound.

The landscape shades
To gold and cinnamon,
And crimson hues burnish
The dogwood leaf,
As maple trees radiate a palette
Unmatched in vibrancy.

As the days unfold,
Our vision sweeps across
Blazing mountains and
Bronzed fields,
A rolling patchwork vista of
Nature's handiwork and
Man's harvest.

Orange pumpkins and seasonal mums
Grace the front stoop,
And in our warm kitchen
Orchard apples,
A fall staple,
Are savored in hand, or
Peeled, sliced, sauced, and baked.

Gingerbread, too, scents the air,
And to accompany
Our evening meal
Acorn squash
Simmers in the oven,
Its scooped center awash
With a delicate mix of
Melted butter, brown sugar, and spice.

Ah, autumn,
This inviting season
Stirs our senses through its unique glory,
And as bird feeders are filled
On a crisp, jacket morning,
The Canada geese fly low above,
Their honking cry and eternal "V"
Eliciting a pause and a prayer:

Godspeed thee on thy flight,
Oh, wondrous bird,
And return next spring
To our cherished land
To awe us with the
Rhythm and routine of thy life.

AUTUMN TIME, AN ENDURING TRUTH

Red bittersweet on the mantle,
An orange pumpkin by the door,
Yellow mums, so bright and cheery,
From the local store.

Each fills my heart with gladness
This autumnal time of year,
Each reminds me to remember
Those I hold especially dear.

For autumn brings reflection,
As deep colors paint the trees,
A time to contemplate the past
While raking up the leaves.

Mother is gone, and Daddy,
Their presence no longer here,
But I always remember their loving ways
Every fall of the calendar year.

For Daddy would rake and burn the leaves
And put an apple on a stick,
And we would roast this juicy treat,
Being careful not to lick.

And Mother would cut some bittersweet
And trim it for her vase,
This lovely "Ode to Autumn"
Gave our room a touch of grace.

Do you, too, have tender memories
Of ones you hold so dear?
Does fall impart the same response,
As you bring its loveliness near?

Autumn is filled with treasured scenes
Of life and moments clear.
To me it is unquestionably
My favorite time of year!

NOVEMBER AND DECEMBER, A HEART'S RESPONSE

Those two glorious months
Which end the calendar year are here:
November, a thankful embrace,
And December, a wondrous light,
Both months a celebration
Of the most sacred and cherished in life.

Thanksgiving Day,
Our revered American holiday,
Fills our thoughts with gratitude
For our country, our family, our faith,
For all the blessings of hearth and home,
A holiday worth the wait.

This sumptuous gathering finds
The fall blaze waning,
The wash of vibrant color now dimmed
And fallen, with accents of soft gold
And Indian red still pleasing the eye, now
Scattered and subtle, replacing the bold.

Tall yellow corn shocks are bundled,
Orange pumpkins are selected, while
Multi-colored apples are baked
Into crisps or pies,
With some pressed into cider or sauce,
All harvested under silvern skies.

The grays and browns of late November
Have become the backdrop

For Holly trees and evergreens,
And as the eleventh month winds down,
Our hearts turn toward December
And the bustle in every town.

This final month of the year is a festival of light,
From the flames of the menorah candles
In celebration of Hanukkah,
To the twinkling lights on house and tree,
Christmas aglow
For all to see.

Despite the purposeful frenzy of
Preparation and purchase,
Our hearts can journey to Bethlehem
With those shepherds of old,
While they follow the bright star,
As the story foretold.

They determinedly seek
The Baby Jesus newborn,
Our Redeemer, our Friend,
Our Enduring Light,
Found in a stable so drear,
He's a wondrous sight!

Yes, the final two months of the year are here
With their gracious, holy themes,
Setting memories ablaze
With holidays past,
Celebrating the Hope and
Joy that *eternally* last.

Dear Heavenly Father,

Thank you for the glory of your world, so alive with the loveliness of color and creation. We stand in awe of all that speaks of you and tells of your love and might. We praise you and rejoice in the wonder and gift of our lives and of those we love. Be with us this November and December and into the New Year. Be our guide and draw us near to you in every way. In Your Holy Name.

Amen.

Invocation Poem and Prayer
Henderson County Genealogical and Historical Society
November 2, 2019

CHRISTMAS TOMORROW
(Written on December 24, 2016)

Yes, the busy days are drawing down,
The end of many trips to town;
The gifts are chosen and under the tree,
Some for you and some for me.

For family far away this year,
Packages sent early draw us near;
Filled with gifts to bring great joy,
Pictures and books and delightful toys.

The Christmas décor shines holy and bright,
With candles, and holly, and colorful lights
That adorn the tree and cast a glow
Upon the nativity nestled below.

Ornaments speak to that moment so clear,
When purchased or received from someone dear;
A twinkling Santa face, hand-made by my mother
Is a treasure to me, one like no other.

December has now too quickly passed,
Can we slow down the days and make them last?
My eyes feast upon each tender scene,
Drawing in the beauty of what it means.

For soon this month will see its end,
As the New Year celebrations send
Us forth into another year,
With memories to cherish, ever so dear.

My prayer for the family and friends I love,
Grateful, I am, to the Lord above,
Who gives me hope and guides my way,
His blessings upon their every day.

TREASURED KEEPSAKES

Christmas and nostalgia are ever entwined, for
as the decorations for tree and table are unpacked,
memories tumble out with the
who, where, when, and how each item came to be,
those treasured keepsakes we long each year to see.

Caressing the Santa face
my mother handmade,
still sequined with sparkle,
o'er a half-century old,
her love for me is the story that's told.

And placed about are
the candles and plates,
the ribbon and holly,
the wreath upon the door;
it's Christmas galore!

Treasured books are unpacked
and handled with care,
their stories old and reaching back
to a time we contemplate with awe,
their simple message a timeless draw.

The nativity set completes most décor,
Mary and Joseph with
Baby Jesus, so tender,
lovingly arranged in a lowly stall,
they tell the reason for it all.

A variation of this poem is found in *Remembering Christmas*.

Wirtz, Ann. "Treasured Keepsakes." In *Remembering Christmas*, compiled and edited by Yvonne Lehman, 126-127. Grace Publishing House, USA, 2019.

Dear Heavenly Father,
Thank you for the wonder and glory of Christmas. This season livens our senses and warms our hearts as we see the treasured beauty that speaks to this holiday alone, as we hear the melodies that uplift with holy thought, and as we share the bounty of your love with others. We ask your mercy and blessing to bring comfort where loss is fresh, where challenge is great, where need is evident. In a world that is desperate for you, may we be your instruments of compassion and love.
In Your Holy Name.
Amen.

Invocation Poem and Prayer
Henderson County Genealogical and Historical Society
December 1, 2018

HOME AND FAMILY

OUR COMMUNITY, A PRAYER IN VERSE

Dear Father,

Home is where our hearts abide,
Our community,
Beloved and treasured,
Nurturing as our roots, new or old,
Grow deep in this resident soil.

Grateful we are for those who've come before,
The builders and creators who,
With extraordinary enterprise,
Championed the best life
For each to achieve.

Regardless the generation,
Challenges are ever present,
For certainly the way is never easy,
But good-hearted faith and the
Determination to succeed do prevail.

Thank You, Dear Lord, for our town,
A vibrant refuge, life-giving with hope,
For our place and time in its history, and
Upon this, our sheltering home,
May Your hand of blessing forever rest.
Amen.

MOM AND DAD

We weren't a family
That shared our private thoughts,
That revealed every struggle,
That sought deep conversation.

We were a family, though,
That kept at our tasks,
That met our obstacles with faith,
That advanced with steady pursuit.

We were a family with Kansas roots,
With a Missouri home, and
With inherited New England stock that combined
With Virginia and Kentucky gumption.

All families have their singular story
With their own fascinating history,
With idiosyncratic ways that set them apart,
With parents who did life as they met it.

Mother, our Dear Mom, born in 1910,
Made a commitment to her family,
Made the chores of home her work,
Made love and sacrifice her offering.

Father, our Dear Dad, born in 1910 as well,
Made the family farm his training ground,
Made his skills propel a tank across Europe,
Made salesmanship his career.

Whether Mother's or Father's Day,
For our parents, loving thankfulness abounds;
For our heritage, pride and humility swell; and
For the gift of life, we are forever grateful.

A MOTHER'S HEART

Oh, the emotion
That rules a mother's heart
And lifts her high
And lays her low
And causes tears
To well and fall.

First, the anticipation
That comes with pregnancy
And imparts great delight
And instills some fear
And causes hope
To arise within.

Then, the birth
That brings precious life
And sets a new course
And fosters bliss
And causes anxiety
To battle against.

Hence, comes the living
That challenges peace
And requires hope
And relies on prayer
And causes joy
To begin anew.

Again, the happening
That ever occurs
And disquiets her heart

And gives her pain
And causes sorrow
To overcome.

Thankfully, there's happiness
That brings a smile
And lights the way
And lifts the lows
And causes pleasure
To embrace.

Surely, the emotion
That rules a mother's heart
And takes her to her knees
And up to the heights
And everywhere in between attests
To her humanity.

DEAREST GRANDS

Of course, I had no idea, really,
It was easy enough to expect
The joy of grandparenthood
To be a marvelous adventure,
And why so ...
Looking at parents with children in tow,
It was easy to grasp the fetching allure
Of grandchildren,
But from afar, who can really be sure.

Then she was born,
Darling little girl, my granddaughter,
And at the wonder of her being,
So breathtaking to behold,
A joy so profound and bright
Radiated as light
From my soul,
With grandchildren,
Adoration abounds untold.

Then he was born,
Darling little boy, my grandson,
And at the wonder of his being,
His beauty did impart
An astonishment so deep
It would forever be
In my heart,
With grandchildren,
It's overwhelming love from the start.

Then begins such treasured times,
It's hard to be apart,
For each visit offers, as they grow,
Books and park swings,
Legos and games,
Crazy Eights, ballet, soccer in the rain,
Cuddles and prayers to make the heart sing,
With grandchildren,
Play is the primary thing.

If born
Of one's own child,
Or another's,
A grandparent is lovingly true,
Faithful each day,
Always remembering to pray
For those sweet, blessed lives, anew,
Yes, love blooms beyond anything
One ever knew.

A variation of this poem is found in *Grandma's Cookie Jar*.

Wirtz, Ann. "Those Darling Grands." In *Grandma's Cookie Jar*, compiled and edited by Yvonne Lehman and Terri Kalfas, 65-66. Grace Publishing House, USA, 2022.

EVER THE MIDWEST

Ever the Midwest abides
In my heart,
Always there,
Forever shaping
My thoughts,
My attitudes,
My longings.

I'm Kansas born and
Missouri bred,
With Wisconsin,
Illinois and
Indiana
Ever brewing the
Mix that is my soul.

With pioneering spirit and
Pragmatic view,
Life is a blend of
Adventure and
Caution,
Prayer and
Resilience.

Now living in the south,
The beautiful North Carolina mountains my home,
The Midwest remains a nostalgic pull,
With its prairie vistas and forested land,
Its farmsteads deep with snow,
Each vibrant season
A yearning memory.

If home has been a base,
A sustainer of roots,
It matters not
Where our ending finds us,
We still exude an enduring vibe,
And mine is
Ever the Midwest.

OUR MOUNTAIN HOME BECKONS

In the Blue Ridge Mountains ...

In the spring, the flowering rhododendron and mountain laurel
Beckon with their exquisite shades of
Pinks and purple,
Rich and deep.

And in the summer, the rolling ridge and high crest
Beckon with their far-reaching undulation of
Blues and green,
Soft with haze.

In the Blue Ridge Mountains ...

In the autumn, the stately forest and deciduous tree
Beckon with their shimmering patchwork of
Reds and gold,
Stitched with pine.

And in the winter, the long vista and slumbering
landscape
Beckon with their peaceful silhouette of
Black against white,
Cold and calm.

Upon this year-round glory, our souls feast,
Beckoned by the beauty of
Mountain top and running stream,
Waterfall and verdant glen.

We rejoice in this corner of the world,
Our Blue Ridge Mountain home,
Beckoning us to stand in wonderment
Before the majesty of God.

FEEDING THE LIVESTOCK

It happens every day,
My morning chore,
The genetics of being
Granddaughter to a farmer
Coming into play and
Sending me forth to
Feed the birds.
This responsibility,
Rain, snow, or shine, I call,
"Feeding the livestock."

While the myriad
Variety of birds
Gracing our feeders
And scratching on the ground
Are my primary care,
The eager stock of squirrels,
Both gray and white,
Are happy beneficiaries
Of the seed I purposely scatter about,
Because they, too, are hungry.

The fluttering and scampering commence
While I putter in the kitchen,
Husband's breakfast and lunch prepared,
The routine accomplished, and after
A kiss goodbye my meal is fixed,
My observant eye ever watching
The antics taking place outside my window,
A lively, animated world
To observe over my breakfast,
Grateful livestock enjoying their own repast.

THE HAY BALES OF SUMMER

My car made its way
Down the winding road,
A lazy jaunt to see the sights
Of farmland and pasture
In the afternoon light.

The land had called
My appreciative heart
To observe summer's lush fare,
In a wholesome adventure
Away from all care.

Garden flowers were rioting,
And farm fields flourishing,
When startling my gaze
As they came into view,
Were hay bales to frankly amaze.

Like massive monuments
They stood, beacons of industry
Gracefully patterned across the field,
Bales of hay, round and mighty,
A wonderfully satisfying yield.

Rolled with grasses,
Clover, Alfalfa, and such,
Ready to be gathered and stored away,
A farmer's work, their livestock to feed
On a distant winter's day.

Formed round or square,
Depending on need, first,
Grasses are cut and sun-dried to cure,
Then raked into windrows long and lean,
Awaiting the baler to make secure.

The day finally comes for "making hay,"
All is ready, critically dry,
The weather sunny and bright,
The baler glides up and down the rows,
Forever a nostalgic sight.

Serendipitous moments occur for all,
Capturing our imagination, giving us pause,
Causing us to think about what we see,
The beauty, the sorrow, the endeavors of man,
The whole of what life can be.

Those hay bales set my thoughts awhirl
About the continuous cycle of life,
A chord resounded deep within,
For the music of a farmer's hard work
Has forever and always been.

EVERYDAY MUSINGS

AND THEN I THOUGHT

It begins in earnest when one turns fifty,
This half-century birthday a milestone
That requires an evaluation, of sorts,
About one's life and how quickly
It has sped by, and how did that happen, btw,
The looking back an inevitable response.

But when one reaches the seventh decade,
The contemplation of one's life includes,
Hopefully, twenty-plus more years to consider,
And, thus, even more wonderment,
And bemusement, and shaking of the head
At how time has escalated to warp speed.

Recounting the events of one's life
Invariably includes musings
About determined decisions
To do, or not to do, something
In which, astonishingly,
The exact opposite actually happened.

Looking back, "And then I thought ..."
Becomes an enlightening catalogue
Of human ignorance and determination
Guided by circumstance,
Changed by revelation, and,
Mercifully, altered by prayer and divine will.

My own personal accounting begins with,
"And then I thought ..."
I'd be a nurse when I grew up,

But high school chemistry intervened,
And the realistic alternative to my poor marks
Was elementary education, and I became a fulfilled teacher.

My next musing involves location, and
All the places I never thought I'd live,
Or never leave, but in the end
Every idea I had in my determined mind
Played out differently,
Much to my surprise.

To be specific, "Decidedly, I thought ..."
I'd never live in the far-away South, then
I'd never leave idyllic Wisconsin, then
I'd never leave bucolic Indiana, and then, yet again,
I'd never leave Wisconsin, my heart love,
And our cozy lake home in the North Woods.

Oh, yes, so much that seemed relatively permanent
Was not, including my marriage, with the death
Of my late husband after thirty-seven years
Of a good and adventuresome marriage,
"And then I thought ..."
I couldn't possibly find someone to marry again.

About faith, "And then I thought ..."
I would never be a Baptist,
Satisfied with the Methodist upbringing
In which I was comfortable
And had learned to love the Lord
With all my heart, for which I'm so grateful!

My life has decidedly and wondrously turned out to be
The direct opposite of everything I ever thought ...

I live in the Blue Ridge Mountains of North Carolina,
I belong to the First Baptist Church of Hendersonville,
And, oh, yes, I am married to
My most precious and perfect second husband, Patrick.

"And then I think…"
Well, maybe it's best not to be so adamant,
For living has its twists, turns, and unknowns
That take us where we never thought we'd go.
So as my heart makes *plans, I know now to pray,
"Thy will be done, Lord, for in Thee I trust."

*Proverbs 16:9 NKJV
A man's heart plans his way,
But the Lord directs his steps.

LIFE IN SNATCHES

Snatching a moment here,
Snatching a moment there,
And filling those brief moments
With a chore or two that receives
An apologetic acknowledgement
That my effort is "a lick and a promise"
Is the way I go.

From trimming and sweeping outside
To dusting and scouring inside,
Every attempt at order and cleanliness
Comes with limited time, as another
Impatient chore demands my attention,
Requiring a simple "good enough"
As I hasten on.

Fortunately, "perfection" isn't required,
As I hum along making loveliness
In seasonal display and garden beauty,
Squinting my eyes often to blur
The scene into a colorful collage,
The imperfections muted into a
Joyfully satisfying design.

Even writing can take on a
Snatch a moment here,
Snatch a moment there reality,
Sitting for a few minutes and penning a few words,
Then up to attend those daily,
And not so daily chores,
That never ending routine that marks our days.

Living life in snatches requires
A certain comfortable self-acceptance
That fosters kindness and humor,
Essentials for the peaceful spirit
Needed to meet daily challenges,
Our best life lived when we also,
Through the day, snatch time to pray.

WHAT MATTERS MOST

What matters most
At the end of a day
When closing thoughts
And final prayers descend
Before sleep overcomes
And awareness slips away?

What makes the greatest
Difference in life
To ease our burdens
And lessen our pain
When troubles arise
And loss is keen?

What is remembered
When years have passed
And hair is gray,
The step less firm
With slower gait
And time has increased its pace?

Simply: faith, family, friends,
Words with profound depth
Held in the heart
With a loving grace born
From a humble spirit
That knows the fragility of life.

What matters most
At the end of our days
Is a life lived with
Compassion that offers words
Of love and hope for family and friends,
To accompany prayers of mercy for them.

SCRAPBOOK MEMORIES

Tucked away
Accumulating age
And distance,
Are photographic memories
Telling a life story
Through a visual lens.

Nestled in
Boxes and drawers
Out of sight,
These pictorial keepsakes of mine
Mark a moment in time
Occurring years long past.

With a sigh
I wonder what to do
With it all,
For surely much is superfluous
And Son and Grands won't have
Room for my memories.

Still, there is
Their genealogy
To be kept,
So, consideration is required
Before I toss and shred
Each recorded moment.

A scrapbook
Provides a solution
To arrange

Memories most relevant and dear,
A legacy of love,
Work, play, abiding faith.

Much is tossed
But much left to peruse,
Ancestry
To ponder, imagining their lives,
Mother and grandmother,
Grandfather and his son.

All the kin
Who have come before us,
Family
With a name or photograph to view,
Life flowing quickly by,
Like a fast-moving stream.

Dear Heavenly Father,
The photographs, letters, stories and documents that
record life give us pause as we stop and study those
rather remarkable mementoes of time – some no
doubt rather unremarkable at the moment of their
inception – but now they are items upon which we
gaze in wonder. Life is a wonderment, indeed, and
for the loveliness of the world around us, and for
the gift of life itself, as evidenced by our recorded
keepsakes, we give you thanks.
Bless this, our annual luncheon, as we gather today
to honor what we treasure: genealogy, history, individual
lives and families, institutions and accomplishments, the
grand and natural beauty of this, our Western North Carolina

Home. For the meal we're about to receive, and for those who prepared it for our nourishment and enjoyment, and for those who are serving to make this time so special, we give you thanks.
In Your Holy Name.
Amen.

Invocation Poem and Prayer
Henderson County Genealogical and
Historical Society Luncheon
August 7, 2021

THE POLLYANNA PRINCIPLE

When but a girl
In the spring of '60,
(An eleven-year-old,
Soon to be twelve,
With compassionate views
And tender sensibilities),
A movie swept into theaters
And into my heart with a principle
From the Holy Word, itself.

Pollyanna, from the book so named,
A 1913 novel by Eleanor H. Porter,
Featured Hayley Mills,
Endearing English star
Who embodied Pollyanna,
The twelve-year-old orphan child
Come to live with her Aunt Polly,
She with a stern and formidable air,
Bound by her own expectations.

A winsome and earnest child,
Pollyanna had taken to heart a biblical truth
Taught by her missionary father,
To choose to play "The Glad Game"
When she faced disappointment,
For certainly something good would be discovered
With the flip of her thinking.
Though ofttimes hidden,
A blessing always awaits, eager to be found.

Loving father, wise to Scripture's message,
He based this game on the *rejoicing texts*
Replete in the Bible, glad passages that
Are answers for the difficulties we encounter,
For they lift our spirits and direct our focus to the good.
Oh, such a blessed truth that changed a community's course,
For Harrington, named for Aunt Polly's family, became
A model of thoughtful kindness because Pollyanna simply
shared
That joy could be found in every disappointment.

Can we, too, embrace this message?
Can we, as well, find joyful solace and hope from the Word of
Grace
Which encourages us to alter a negative perspective?
Proverbs 17:22 (NIV) proclaims the why, "A cheerful heart is
good medicine,
But a crushed spirit dries up the bones,"
While 1 Thessalonians 5:16-18 (NIV) provides the way,
"Rejoice always, pray continually, give thanks in all
circumstances;
For this is God's will for you in Christ Jesus,"
An attitude-changing truth from the One who
overcomes all.

A SIGH

With a distinct release of breath,
Air escaping from parted lips,
Upper body contracting visibly,
Posture slumping slightly,
A sigh has left my body,
And it feels so good!

A peaceful sensation
Carries anxiety away,
And relief floods my soul,
As the rhythmic inhale then
Continues the natural back and forth
Of effortless existence.

Revelatory one day
Were the deep sighs
From Husband and me
Before our morning prayer,
And while observed before,
This moment was a decided aha!

Before we pray, we sigh,
A healing release that ushers
In a spirit of calm
As we come to the Lord,
Our hearts now swept to experience
The joy of His loving presence.

Then, when dear friend Leanna
Came for coffee and yummies
One morning, as she often does ...

Our time to right life's tilting course ...
She, too, sighed before her prayer,
And the power of the sigh was clear.

Sighs may escape our lips
At other times, undoubtedly,
But a sigh before prayer
Is a willing surrender,
As we turn our anxious minds to Him,
Eager, hopeful, and grateful to receive His peace.

LOGIC VS REALITY

Oh, how my mind
Sees the world
And personal situations
Through a lens that
Demands a logical
Response and outcome.
And, yet, how this
Seems rarely to occur,
Much to my surprise
And disappointment.

"Anything logical
Is probably unrealistic
At this point,"
I opined with a smile to
Laura, Fran, and Rosemary,
My *Friends of Gladys Taber* group,
Their solutions
Logical, reasonable,
And kindly offered to improve
Realities mused over cups of tea.

And how is it that
What seems reasonable
In life is passed over
With other actions that
Leave us shaking our heads
And wondering, "Why?"
As choices are made
In other ways,
With outcomes both good
And troubling?

It's truly
A curious perplexity,
One that requires a deeper
Look at human nature
With, ironically,
A logical and realistic understanding,
And even patient acceptance of
Individual personalities,
Their genetics at work
Within the sphere of their environment.

Fortunately, there is
An answer for my troubled thoughts
In prayer and The Word so clear,
My sources for profound hope and solace,
Where victory is gained over despair,
And my heart is soothed, for
I purposely, instead, *take captive every thought*,
Understanding **if there be any virtue [or] praise,
I'm to *think on these things*,
And, thus, am saved from a world of heartache.

*2 Corinthians 10:5 NIV
**Philippians 4:8 KJV

OUR DUTIES

History holds
A keen fascination,
With its stories
And realities
A record of life itself,
Facts revealed in a straightforward,
Yet usually astounding,
Oh, my goodness sort of way.

A bit of history
Recently caught
My attention and
Gave great pause,
As it provided a clarity that
Resonated deeply
With its expressed truths,
Both simple and profound.

Christmas 1937,
And King George VI
Gave a radio address
To the United Kingdom
And the Dominions of
The British Commonwealth,
The nations he served
From 1936 until his death in 1952.

A year on the throne
Following his brother's abdication
The previous December,
With his formal coronation in May,

George VI was the father of
The future queen and
Longest reigning British monarch,
Her Majesty Queen Elizabeth II.

From a young age,
A severe stammer
Had plagued the King
And made public speaking
An agonizing ordeal.
Remediation began in 1926 with
Australian speech and language therapist,
Lionel George Logue.

With techniques in breathing and
Intense concentrated practice,
The King learned how to successfully
Manage his speech impediment,
His determination bolstered
By the demands of his unsought role,
His public pronouncements becoming
Carefully precise and reassuring.

The King's Christmas broadcast
Was delivered in this manner,
His words of encouragement and hope
More necessary than ever,
For with the world experiencing
Shadows of enmity and fear,
He urged all to *turn to the message*
That Christmas brings, of peace and goodwill.

This *immortal message,*
Should indeed be

The keystone of our daily lives, he affirmed,
But what pierced my heart most of all,
Because it's so easy to complain and
And chafe at our everyday tasks and demands,
Are the simple and yet profound words that followed,
Attitude changing words that shift one's thinking.

And so to all of you,
Whether at home among your families,
As we are, or in hospital,
Or at your posts
Carrying out those duties
That cannot be left undone*,*
We send our Christmas greetings,
And wish you God's blessing.

All history has a back story,
And digging into
The elusive realities of people's lives
For the how and why of historical
And personal fact is an adventure
From which we can take both heart and hope,
For it shows the hard commonality of life,
And encourages us to resolutely "Carry On!"

A DESPERATE MESS

There are numerous places
In my home
Where a mess prevails,
Yet words of encouragement
Are sincere when my hands
Quickly righten a bit of it,
Though my rueful endeavor
Only comes with a light promise.

One area, however, demanded
Attention to the disorder,
So terribly out of hand it was,
My poor sock drawer,
A desperate mess,
Always opened with trepidation,
Knowing the contents were stuffed
To the top and ready to overflow.

An afternoon was set aside
To tackle the behemoth,
The recorded television programs
Of historical merit or
Escapist entertainment on the ready,
For working through one's sock drawer
Requires time and patience
To sort, pitch, and carefully organize.

The mission was accomplished
One snowy afternoon,
When the flakes fell lazily,

Yet persistent,
Much like me,
I thought, for with age
I'm less intent on my chores,
Though I do accomplish them in the end.

I'M HERE BECAUSE

I'm here because ...
Why am I here?
In the pantry,
In the bedroom,
In the closet,
In the ...
Well, it doesn't matter
Where I find myself,
Because sometimes
I arrive at my destination
And can't remember
Why I'm there!

I puzzle over the matter,
Tracing my prior
Actions and steps,
And fortunately, for now,
Can usually recall
Quite quickly,
And thankfully,
The reason for where I am,
The very why
I've gone there,
And feel grateful that,
Once more, I could remember.

FAMILY LINES

Curiosity about
Who we are, and
Why we do as we do
Lies behind our
Earnest desire and quest
To determine the
Greats and grands
Who have given birth
To our family lines upon this earth.

Our genealogical adventure
Takes us far and wide
As we delve into history
Recorded as true,
Research demanding
An in-depth look
To compare what's known
When facts don't jive,
Seeking accuracy about our lives.

So many lines
Excitedly beckon,
Limbs reaching out and
Deep into the past
Into the realm of unknown lore
Where ancient kin exist,
Discovering origins and ancestors
And the choices they made,
Marveling at life, this very day.

Some branches pique
Our interest more,
A mysterious lure
For an eager venture,
My Scottish/English roots
An intriguing draw, unveiling
Castles, Ladies, Knights,
Those brave who crossed the ocean vast,
Our heritage a gift from the valiant past.

It's a curious thing,
Our response to life,
Who we are, and
Why we do as we do,
We search family lines
For reasons that explain
Our inclination for this or that,
Finding fascinating clues
For the life we choose.

GENEALOGICAL SOCIETIES, A PRAYER OF DEDICATION

Dear Heavenly Father,

We gather this morning,
those of us who relish
the past,
the old ways, and
the old days.

We research and remember
those kin and kind who came before,
the ones who established
the first homes and farms,
the founders of businesses and communities.

We honor life upon life,
the genealogy
of a nation and a state,
of a county and a town,
of a place called home.

We marvel at accomplishments and facts
preserved for the finding
in old newspapers and wills,
in Bibles and diaries,
in court records and documents.

We unearth photographs and stories, old and frayed,
revealing who we are as a people,
by feature or manner,
by skill or bent,
by faith lived out.

For these treasures uncovered
and for those yet to be found,
we give thanks,
we pray in Your Name,
we say, "Amen."

Prayer of Dedication June 1, 2013
Henderson County Genealogical and Historical Society
Dr. George A. and Evelyn Masden Jones, Founders

THE OLD PHOTOGRAPH

Give me an old photograph, any day,
Life captured in black and white;
The lines, the edges, and curves
Clearly defined by the dark and the light ...

The natural world: a seeming silhouette, simple and pure, wild
and epic;
The structure: a declarative statement, sturdy and bold, grand
and poor;
The people: a reflective study, somber and joyful, family and
stranger.

Our curiosity taking hold,
We pause to contemplate
What life was like in those days so long ago.
How were challenges met?

Did faith make the difference, as now for some?
Our imagination is set to wondering,
For color gives clues and color gives facts,
But black and white is a mystery waiting to be told.

Dear Heavenly Father,
Life has many mysteries that arouse our curiosity.
When we contemplate the past through the old
photograph, through the old writing, through the
old keepsake, we are struck by the scope of time and by all
that has happened ... and by all that has changed. We are
grateful that you alone are unchanging, that your love is ever

constant, and that as events unfold, and time marches on, and mysteries mount, we can trust in you. Thank you for clues, for memories, for faith that protects and saves in the darkest hour. Thank you for life abundant through the ages, the thread of life that has overcome war, famine and disease. As we contemplate the past, we pray for your continued guidance and mercy on the future.

In Your Holy Name.

Amen.

Invocation and Prayer
Henderson County Genealogical and Historical Society
April 11, 2015

THE OLD THING

A book, its pages yellow and fragile,
A spoon, its silver engraved with life,
A utensil, its service clear and true,
A map, its courses long detailed,
A trunk, its contents now unknown,
An album, its photos of lives untold,
A face, its eyes a portal to muse,
A mouth, its line a somber mystery,
A dress, its form petite and frail,
A picture, its scene a timeless marvel,
A Bible, its family record kept,
A document, its legal proclamation sure,
A newspaper, its daily news proclaimed,
A story, its account a moment retold,
An artifact, its curiosity a guess,
A February, its first Saturday a sharing,
A gathering, its program our "Show and Tell,"
A blessing, its source the genealogy that binds,
A revealing, its wonder bringing us back,
Again, to witness the old thing.

Dear Heavenly Father,
May we always treasure "the old thing," that item
or story that captures our imagination and causes
us to wonder about life in "the old days." We thank
you for our country, our heritage, our genealogical
roots that astound and give pride. We are a blessed people,
and for that we give you thanks.

In Your Holy Name.
Amen.

Invocation and Prayer
Henderson County Genealogical and Historical Society
February 1, 2014

Printed in the United States
by Baker & Taylor Publisher Services